LITTLE BIG BOOKS

ALL ABOUT DOGS

SUE NASH

Editor: Trisha Pike Designer: Jacky Cowdrey
Picture Researcher: Kathy Brandt

Purnell

1 THE DOG'S ANCESTORS

45 million years ago there lived an animal called Miacis. It was a small creature with a long body, a long tail and short legs. It could run quite fast and also climb trees. These things made it easy for the Miacis to hunt other animals for food.

Over millions of years the descendants of Miacis slowly changed their shape and way of living until a new kind of animal developed. This animal was Cynodictis.

Cynodictis did not climb trees like

Above: Cynodictis.

Above: Lycaon.

Below: There are nine kinds of wolf.

Below: The skull of a wolf.

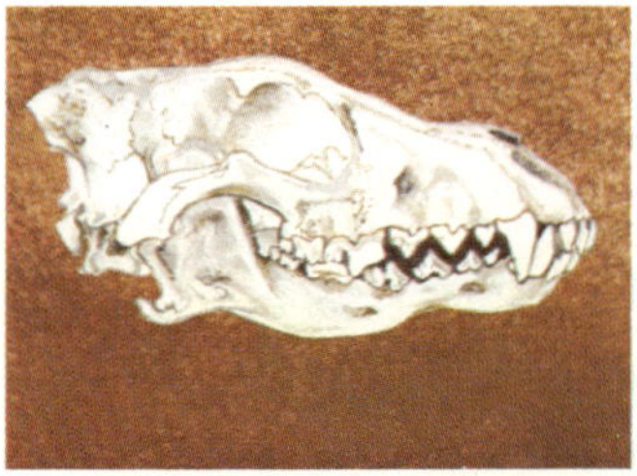

The dog family went through many changes before dogs look as they do today.

Above: Borophagus.

Miacis but it still hunted for its food. It could run much faster than Miacis because its legs were longer.

After Cynodictis came three different kinds of animal. Each of them was a kind of dog.

The first was Lycaon. From Lycaon came the African Hunting dogs. The second was Borophagus. The hyena and jackal are descended from this animal. The third was Tomarctus. The fox and the wolf came from this type of dog. It is possible that the first real dogs are descended from both the wolf and the jackal. No one is really sure.

Left: Tomarctus looked more like a modern dog.

Below: The skull of a jackal.

Below: The jackal barks and howls, as a dog does.

2 MAN'S BEST FRIEND

The very first dogs still hunted for their food. They roamed around in packs and were frightened of people. Then, about 20,000 years ago these dogs began to creep near people's camp fires. They liked the warmth. They also found food lying around the camps.

Dogs and people began to get used to each other. Soon the dogs were helping people in many ways. For example, they barked at anything which came near the camp. This warned people of danger.

Dogs also helped men hunt for

Below: Sheepdog herding, likely as the first dogs did.

animals. The dogs would track animals by sniffing the ground and following the smell.

Later on, people began to keep sheep and goats. The dogs would herd them together and stop them from wandering away. The dogs also fought off wolves when they came too near the herd. In return for this work people gave the dogs food, care and shelter. This was how people and dogs became friends.

Dogs were the first animals to be domesticated. They were the first to live with people and be looked after.

Above: Dogs were man's first domestic animals. They probably guarded the caves.

3 THE FAMILIES

Most breeds of dog belong to one of six families.

The first of these is the Spitz group. Their ears are pointed and stand up straight. They have tails which curl up over their backs.

Next there is the Sheepdog family. Their coats are the sort which keep out cold and damp. They are clever dogs and enjoy being with their owners.

Dogs of the Greyhound family are

1. Siberian Husky. 2. Cairn Terrier. 3. Deerhound.

able to run very fast. This is because they are thin, light and have long legs. When they hunt they use their eyes and not their noses.

In the Hound family are the dogs with very long ears that hang down. These dogs are the best at following smells with their noses. They are also good at obeying orders.

Nearly all the very big dogs belong to the Mastiff family. Dogs of this kind have wide faces and look very strong.

Small breeds of dogs with wiry coats belong to the Terrier family. These dogs get excited very easily and love to show off.

4. Bloodhound. 5. Old English Sheepdog. 6. Dalmatian.

4 GUN DOGS

Above: A Golden Retriever brings back a shot pheasant to its owner.

Gun dogs are taught to help people who go shooting. These dogs find and fetch ducks and rabbits for their owners. Pointers, Spaniels and Retrievers are all gun dogs.

The Pointer can smell the trail of a bird by sniffing the air. When the Pointer knows where the bird is, it stands quite still. It then points at the bird with its nose. At the same time it lifts one paw. This is how its owner knows where the bird is.

Above: This Pointer points at a bird with its nose.

Left: Spaniels scare birds from out of their hiding places.

A Spaniel can run through long grass and undergrowth very quickly, because it is small. As it runs it scares birds and animals out of their hiding places. This is called "flushing". The dog's owner can then see them and aim his gun at them.

The Retriever's job is to find birds and animals after they have been shot. It then brings them to its owner. This is called "retrieving" which is how this dog got its name.

All the gun dogs have very soft mouths. Their lips hang a long way over their teeth. This means that when they carry anything in their mouths they do not make tooth marks in it.

Above: An R.A.F. police dog.

Above: An Alsatian dog in the Alps helping to rescue people trapped under a fall of snow.

5 WORKING DOGS

Dogs work hard for people in a lot of different ways. One of the most important jobs they do is guiding the blind. The dog must be able to lead the blind person through crowds and along streets. It is taught how to cross roads safely.

Most police forces also use dogs to help them in their work. Police dogs are trained to catch criminals

by chasing them and grabbing them with their mouths. Alsatians do this job as they are big and strong.

A trained Sheepdog is a very useful working dog. It is able to round up sheep and cattle.

Life would be very hard for the Eskimos without their Husky dogs. These dogs pull sledges over the ice carrying people, furs and food.

In the Alps people can be trapped under snow and ice. Nowadays, Alsatians are mainly used for rescue jobs. They are trained to be able to find people who are trapped even under very deep snow.

Above: A guide dog taking care of its owner.

Above: A sledge pulled by Huskies is the best way to travel in snow.

6 TOY DOGS

The toy dogs are the very small breeds. At one time many toy dogs were used to catch rats. Now they are usually kept as pets.

The owners of toy dogs often like to dress them up. Pretty collars, jackets and even boots are sold for these dogs.

The Yorkshire Terrier nearly always wears a bow. This is tied around the long hair on top of its head. Sometimes its fur is curled.

Poodles have to have their fur

Right: Clothes for toy dogs.
Below: A Japanese Chin looks very like a Pekinese.

Above: A Yorkshire Terrier.

Above: A Poodle having its fur clipped in a Poodle parlor.

Below: You can buy ear muffs, boots and a coat for your dog.

clipped. The clipping must be done very carefully. The Poodle should look as if it is wearing a wig, a cloak and short trousers.

Pomeranians were the favorite toy dogs about a hundred years ago. Then Pekinese were brought from China. They quickly became the new favorites. Both Pomeranians and Pekinese have to be brushed daily.

At one time ladies would carry a Papillon about with them. They thought that this toy spaniel would keep away stomach-ache.

7 THE PERFORMERS

Nearly all the small dogs enjoy showing off. They like learning tricks and doing them in front of an audience.

The dog usually chosen for circus acts is the Poodle. This is because it looks pretty. Also it moves daintily and is very clever.

Although dogs are afraid of fire they can be trained to jump through a hoop of fire. This makes a wonderful circus act.

Greyhounds and Whippets are famous as fast runners. The Ancient

Racing Greyhounds chase a toy hare around the track.

Left: Poodles are often used in circus acts.

Below: Jumping through fire is difficult for dogs.

Romans used to like Greyhound racing. Today it is still a favorite sport. The Greyhounds chase around a grass track trying to catch a toy hare. The dog which wins the race makes a lot of money for its owner. Whippets are also used in races of this kind.

Dogs of all kinds are used in films. They are also used a lot in television advertisements.

All over the world dogs are entertaining people in all these different ways.

Right: A Border Collie and (left) a Lurcher. These dogs are both cross-breeds. The Lurcher is a gypsy dog.

Below: Mongrels make very good pets as they are good-natured. But you never know to what size they will grow.

8 MONGRELS

A mongrel is a dog which does not belong to any breed. Mongrels can be any size, shape or color. This is because their parents and grandparents were all different types of dogs. Dogs whose parents and grandparents were all the same breed are called purebreds.

Mongrels can do the jobs that working dogs do. Most mongrels, though, are kept as pets. There is no way of telling how a mongrel puppy

Above: A Kelpie runs along the backs of sheep to round them up.

will look when it grows up. It is a mixture of different breeds and so it may become a big dog or a little dog. It may become a long or short haired dog, a brave dog or a shy one.

There are some dogs which are not mongrels or purebreds. They are cross-breeds. The Lurcher can be a mixture of Greyhound with Deerhound, Whippet, Sheepdog and Retriever. Each Lurcher looks a little different depending on the mixture. Many hundreds of years ago the Border Collie and the Kelpie were also a mixture of different breeds of dog. But now all Border Collies are alike and all Kelpies are alike. Some people think they are purebreds.

9 LARGE, SMALL AND CURIOUS

The biggest dog is the Irish Wolfhound. When it stands up on its back legs it is as tall as a man. Because it is so big it can look fierce, but it is very sweet-tempered.

The Pyrenean Mountain Dog is another huge dog. It is very gentle like the Irish Wolfhound. Both these dogs were once kept by shepherds. Their job was to scare away wolves from the sheep.

The smallest dogs in the world

Below: 1. A Mexican Hairless. 2. A Rough Collie. 3. A Pembroke Corgi. 4. An Irish Wolfhound. 5. A Basset Hound.

are Chihuahuas. They are about 5 inches high. Rich families in Mexico kept lots of these tiny dogs.

Another dog from Mexico is the Mexican hairless. These dogs have no fur at all. They were used to keep sick people warm in bed. The Chinese Crested Dog is also bald except for a tuft of hair on its head.

A few other dogs are unusual in one way or another. The Chow dog is odd because it has a blue tongue. The Basenji dog cannot bark. Instead it makes a strange yodel.

Above: The Chow was a working dog in ancient China. It has a blue tongue.

Below: 6. A Chihuahua. 7. A Pyrenean Mountain Dog. 8. A Chinese Crested Dog. 9. An Alsatian. 10. A Spaniel.

Above: The film star Collie who played Lassie.

All over the world children and grown-ups alike enjoy films with dogs in them. Some dogs are liked so much that they become famous.

The "Lassie" films made the Collie dog a film star. Collie dogs are now often called Lassie dogs.

The film "Hound of the Baskervilles" made Irish Wolfhounds famous. In the film an Irish Wolfhound had to pretend to be very fierce to scare people.

Walt Disney's dog cartoons are well-known. "101 Dalmatians" and "Lady and the Tramp" made dogs and puppies even more lovable.

Below: Laika was a Russian Terrier and the first to travel in space.

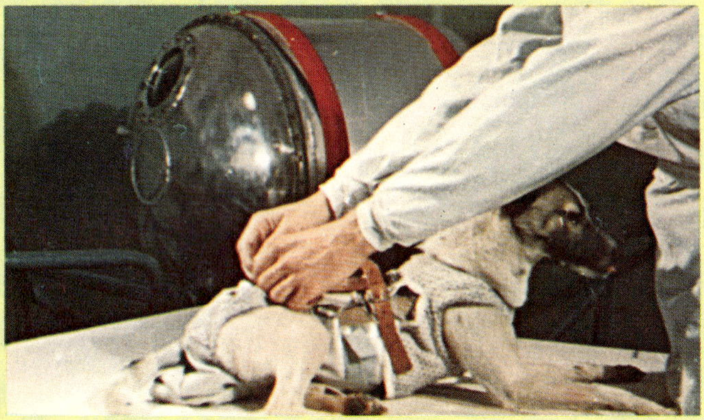

Below: This painting of a dog is a record company's trademark.

Above: A still from the Walt Disney film "Lady and the Tramp".

Pluto was the first of Disney's cartoon dogs. He got into a lot of trouble and made people laugh because he was so stupid.

Many dogs are well-known from advertisements. A famous make of whisky likes to show two dogs as its trademark. One is a black Scottish Terrier and the other is a white West Highland Terrier.

A Terrier named Laika became famous for a much more special reason. In 1957 she was chosen as the first dog to travel in space.

11 PUPPIES

Puppies are looked after by their mother until they are eight weeks old. The mother dog gives them food, care and warmth. When she needs to carry them she picks them up in her mouth.

Choosing a puppy must be done very carefully. There are a lot of things to think about.

The puppy must be looked after every single day. It must be fed and played with. It must sleep in a box or a basket. This must be kept clean and cosy. Later on it will need a collar and leash. When it has grown up a little it will have to be taken out

Above: After three weeks a puppy can eat solid foods.

1

2

3

for walks. All these things take time and money.

When picking up a puppy make sure it feels safe and secure.

All puppies love to play but they also need a lot of sleep.

At first the puppy will not be used to being away from its mother. It will probably feel lonely for the first few nights. It is a good idea to put a hot water bottle in the puppy's bed. Make sure the bottle is wrapped up well. This will help to comfort the lonely puppy.

Puppies should always look happy and want to make friends. They should have cold, wet noses and bright, clear eyes.

Left: It is very important to pick up your puppy correctly. 1. Do not pick it up by its front legs. 2. Do not pick it up underneath its front legs. 3. This is the correct way. Always support the puppy's weight from underneath.

Below: Every dog should have a warm, dry bed of its own.

12 TRAINING

The first thing a puppy should get used to is its collar and leash. The collar should have the owner's name and address on it in case the dog gets lost.

The puppy will take a while to get used to its leash. When it first wears the leash, take the puppy only around the house and yard. Do not let it go along roads just yet.

The puppy should not pull on its leash. It should walk quietly by the

Below: Your dog should be trained always to walk at your heel.

Below: Tell your dog to "sit". At the same time put one hand under its chin and press down on its rump with the other.

Left: Dogs learn easily to walk properly. But sometimes it helps to go to dog training classes.

side of its owner. If it is difficult to make it walk properly then it is a good idea to take the puppy to dog training classes.

When a puppy looks as though it wants to go to toilet it should be put into the yard. It will soon learn always to go to toilet outside.

It is quite easy to get a puppy to sit. Put one hand under its head. With the other hand press gently down on the bottom of its back. Tell the puppy to "Sit". When the puppy has sat down praise and pet him.

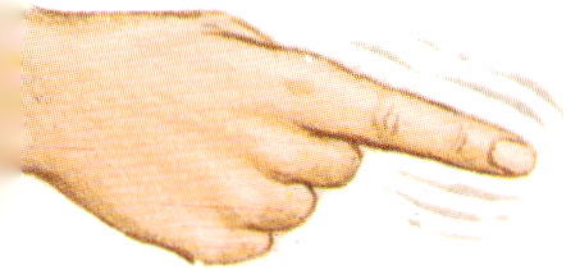

Whenever a puppy or a dog is doing wrong it should be told "No". Use a loud, firm voice to say this. As soon as it stops doing wrong pat it.

Left: If your dog does something wrong tell it off right away. You should say "No" in a loud, firm voice.

13 CARING FOR YOUR PET

Above: Dogs with long ears should have the flap cleaned.

A dog should be taken to a vet when it is three months old. The vet will make sure the dog will not catch hard-pad or distemper. These are very serious dog illnesses.

It is usually easy to tell when a dog is well or sick. The fur of a healthy dog is glossy and its eyes are bright. A sick dog has dull fur and dull eyes. When a dog is ill it should be taken to a vet.

Sometimes dogs need to have their ears cleaned. A pad of cotton is the best thing to use. Only the flap of

Left: Dogs with long hair should be brushed every day; otherwise the fur becomes knotted. If that happens it becomes painful for the dogs and the knots have to be cut away by a vet. The fur then looks ragged.

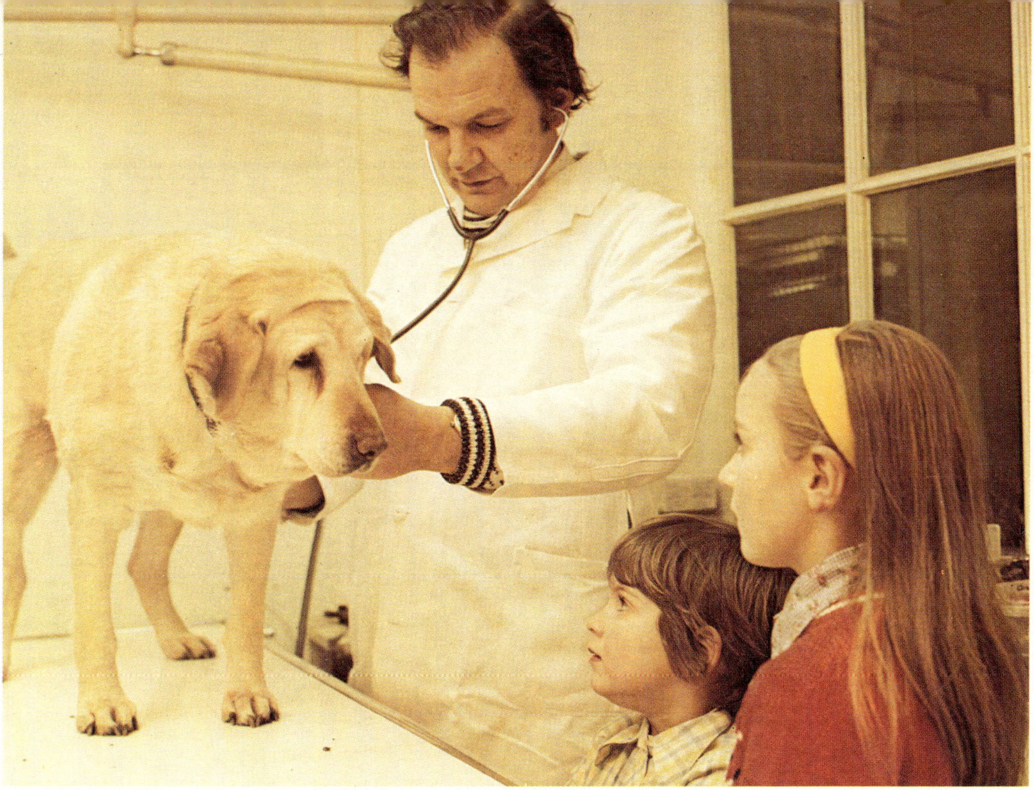

Above: If your dog is ill take it to a vet.

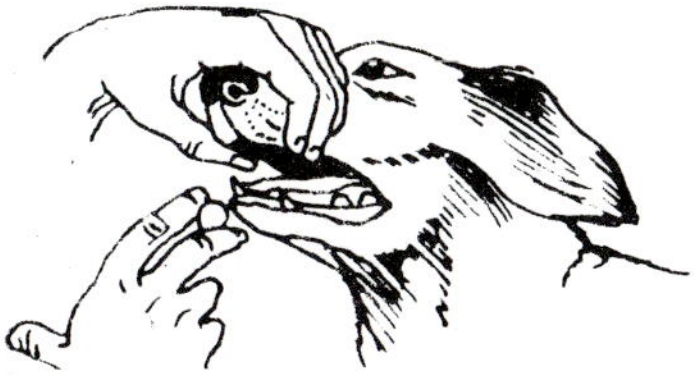

When giving your dog pills hold its snout, pressing inward. When its mouth opens, tilt its head back and pop in the pill.

the ear should be cleaned. Never the inside of the ear.

On the inside of a dog's leg is the dew-claw. It is just above the paw. Sometimes these claws get very long. A vet will cut the claws. Most dogs have good teeth if they are not given sweet things to eat. Big, raw bones help to keep their teeth strong and clean.

It is important to find out how much food to give a dog. A bowl of clean water should always be where a dog can find it.

OWNING A DOG

Looking after a dog is a very important job. It has to be done in the right way. Very big dogs should not be kept in small houses or apartments. They need plenty of room to move. No dog should be left by itself all day. It gets bored and lonely.

All dogs need as many walks as possible. They should live near parks or fields. They like places where they can safely be let off their

Above: A dog comb, rubber bone, brush, ball and collar.

leashes. Then they can sniff and wander about where they want to.

Dogs enjoy being friends with people. Most dogs get on well with everyone in the family. But some dogs like to have a best friend. These dogs pick out someone as their special owner.

Games and toys give a dog a lot of fun. They like running after balls and sticks. They also like to join in chasing games. These games must be played only in places where there is no traffic.

Below: Make sure your dog has plenty of exercise. It will enjoy long walks and running after sticks.

Above: This Maltese Terrier is being made ready to go on show.

Above: Two Afghans wait for their turn in the show.

15 DOG SHOWS

In some countries dog shows are held so as to choose the best dog of each breed. All Spaniels are shown together, all Poodles, all Bulldogs and so on. The dogs are tested to see how perfect they are. Prizes are given to the dogs which win.

Before a dog is taken to a show its owner makes it look its very best. It is bathed and brushed. Its claws and teeth are polished and cleaned.

When a dog arrives at a show it is put on a platform. In this way people

can get close to look at it. They can then see its good and bad points.

The dogs are next taken to be tested by the judges. The dogs are walked around a ring by their owners. Every dog must be well behaved.

The judges then look at each dog in turn. They check the way it stands and how it walks. They also look at its teeth and eyes. At last the judges say which dogs they think are the best. Silver cups and medals are given to the top dogs. Dogs which win the first prizes are champions.

Below: These Spaniels are being judged at a dog show.

Below: A West Highland White Terrier with the prizes it has won.

WORDS YOU MAY NOT KNOW

Advertisement A notice in newspapers or on television or radio which gives information about anything from cars for sale to a new kind of toothpaste.

Audience The people who watch a film or see a play being performed.

Breed A group of dogs which have the same general features. The Mastiff breed, for example, is well-known for the power of scent.

Champion The dog judged to be the best in its breed out of all the dogs put on show.

Criminal A person who does something against the laws of his country.

Domesticated A dog or other animal that is used to being with people.

Entertain To give pleasure, such as when a dog performs in a circus.

Judge A person who decides the winner in a contest or competition.

Platform A stage on which anything stands or where a person performs to an audience.

Prey An animal that is hunted for food.

Trademark A mark used by a company to insure that people will recognize its products.

Traffic The passing of vehicles along a road.

Vet Animal doctor.